MOLLIE KATZEN'S RECIPES

Desserts

TEN SPEED PRESS
Berkeley | Toronto

I've tried to include something for just about everyone in this fun collection of desserts.

There are several fruit pies, a rich cheesecake as well as a light one, and some traditional cookies that keep well in a tin (and are always useful to have on hand) — as well as cakes, plain and fancy, and puddings and mousses — highfat, lowfat, and in between.

In addition to end-of-meal fare, many of these preparations are lovely additions to afternoon tea or Sunday brunch.

I hope there is something here that will please just about everyone, and that these recipes sweetly enhance and expand your repertoire.

 PANTRY NOTES

In case you need a brief explanation of some of the ingredients used in this book:

BUTTER: Use unsalted or lightly salted.

DAIRY PRODUCTS: You can use lowfat (and often nonfat) everything: milk, cottage cheese, ricotta, sour cream, evaporated milk, yogurt, etc. Soy or rice milk can frequently be substituted.

EXTRACTS (VANILLA, ALMOND, ETC.): Use pure only.

FLOURS: Unless otherwise specified, use unbleached white flour.

FROZEN FOODS: I frequently tested these recipes with frozen unsweetened fruit (berries, cherries, etc.), with great success, when fresh were unavailable.

JUICES: Use fresh-squeezed lemon, lime, or orange juice in these recipes whenever possible.

SWEETENERS: To varying degrees, sugar, brown sugar, honey, and real maple syrup are used in the desserts. In some cases they are interchangeable. This is indicated on individual recipes.

Table of Contentment

• • • Moosewood Fudge Brownies • • •

15 minutes to make
25 minutes to bake

Yield: a 9x13-inch panful

On a brownie-intensity scale of 1 to 10, these are about an 11;
in other words, not for the faint-hearted. You should probably
have some good vanilla or coffee ice cream on hand, or you'll
find yourself running out to the store to get some as soon as you
take a bite, and this will rudely interrupt your dessert hour.

butter for the pan

5 oz. (5 squares) unsweetened chocolate
½ lb. (2 sticks) butter or margarine, softened
1¾ cups (packed) light brown sugar (white sugar also ok)
5 eggs
1½ tsp. vanilla extract
1 cup flour (use ¾ cup for fudgier brownies)

MANY OPTIONAL EMBELLISHMENTS:
1 cup chopped walnuts or pecans
1 tsp. freshly grated orange rind
½ tsp. cinnamon
a small ripe banana, mashed
2 to 4 Tbs. strong black coffee

1 cup semisweet chocolate chips
OR anything else you might think of
OR, for purists, none of the above

1) Butter a 9 X 13-inch baking pan. Preheat oven to 350°F.

2) Gently melt the chocolate. Let it cool for about 10 minutes.

3) Cream the butter and sugar in a medium-sized bowl until light and fluffy.

4) Add the eggs, one at a time, beating well after each. Stir in the vanilla.

5) Stir constantly as you drizzle in the melted chocolate. After all the chocolate is in, beat well for a minute or two.

6) Stir in flour and possible embellishments. Mix just enough to blend thoroughly.

7) Spread the batter into the prepared pan. Bake 20 to 25 minutes, or until a knife inserted into the center comes out clean. Cut into squares while still hot, then allow to cool for at least 10 minutes, if you can wait that long.

Date-Nut Cake

Preparation time: 15 minutes
Baking time: 40 to 50 minutes
Yield: about 6 servings

butter and flour for the pan
3 eggs, separated and
   at room temperature
1/4 cup sugar
1/2 tsp. vanilla extract
1/3 cup flour
1/4 tsp. salt
3/4 cup very finely chopped nuts
   (walnuts, almonds, or pecans)
1 cup chopped dates

TOPPING
1/2 pint heavy cream or 1 cup ricotta cheese
1/2 tsp. vanilla extract
2 to 3 Tbs. powdered sugar (or, to taste)

1) Preheat oven to 350°F. Generously butter and flour a 9-inch round pan.

2) In a medium-sized bowl, beat the egg whites with an electric mixer at high speed until stiff but not dry.

3) In a second medium-sized bowl, beat the egg yolks with sugar and vanilla for several minutes — until smooth and thick.

4) Stir the flour, salt, nuts, and dates into the yolk mixture and blend well. Gently fold in the beaten egg whites.

5) Transfer to the prepared pan and bake for 40 minutes, or until the surface of the cake springs back when touched lightly. Remove from the oven and allow to cool in the pan. Invert onto a serving plate.

6) Combine the cream or ricotta with vanilla and powdered sugar, and whip to your favorite consistency. Spread over the top of the cake, and chill. Serve cold.

Orange Cake

Preparation time: 30 minutes
Baking time: 50 to 60 minutes
Allow time to cool and glaze

Yield: 1 large cake,
    serves 12 to 16

butter for the pan
1 1/2 cups (3 sticks) butter,
   softened
1 3/4 cups sugar
4 eggs

1 tsp. grated orange rind
1 tsp. vanilla extract
3 cups flour
1 Tbs. baking soda
1/2 tsp. salt

1 cup sour cream or yogurt
1/2 cup orange juice
} whisked together

ORANGE GLAZE:
1/2 cup orange juice
1 to 2 Tbs. sugar
1 Tbs. lemon juice
optional: 2 to 3 Tbs. dry sherry or orange liqueur

1) Preheat oven to 350°F. Butter a 10-inch tube or bundt pan.

2) In a large bowl, beat together the butter and sugar until light and fluffy.

3) Add the eggs, one at a time, beating well after each.

4) Stir in the orange rind and vanilla. Set aside.

5) Sift together the dry ingredients in a separate bowl. Add this to the butter mixture alternately with the combined sour cream (or yogurt) and orange juice, beginning and ending with the dry ingredients. Mix by hand after each addition — just enough to combine well.

6) Turn into the prepared pan. Bake 50 to 60 minutes, or until a knife inserted all the way down comes out clean. Cool for about 15 minutes, then invert onto a plate. Allow to cool completely.

7) Combine the glaze ingredients in a small saucepan and bring to a boil. Lower heat and simmer uncovered for about 3 minutes. Pour the hot glaze onto the cooled cake. Let stand at least 10 minutes before slicing.

Ukrainian
Poppy Seed
Cake

Preparation time: 30 minutes

Baking time: 40 minutes

Yield: about 10 servings

$\frac{3}{4}$ cup poppy seeds
1 cup milk
butter or margarine for the pan, plus
$\frac{1}{2}$ lb. (2 sticks) butter or margarine
1 cup sugar (white or light brown)
3 eggs
2 cups flour

1 Tbs. baking powder
1 tsp. baking soda
$\frac{1}{2}$ tsp. salt
1 tsp. vanilla extract
3 Tbs. lemon juice
1 tsp. lemon rind
OPTIONAL: Orange Glaze
(page 10)

1) Place poppy seeds and milk in a small saucepan. Heat just to the boiling point, but remove from heat before it actually boils. (This is called scalding.) Set aside and allow to cool for at least 15 minutes.

2) Preheat oven to 350°F. Butter a 10-inch tube or bundt pan.

3) Cream the butter and sugar in a large mixing bowl. Add eggs, one at a time, beating well after each.

4) Sift together the dry ingredients in a separate bowl. Add this to the butter mixture alternately with the poppyseed-milk, beginning and ending with the dry mixture. Stir just enough to blend thoroughly, adding the vanilla, lemon juice, and lemon rind at the end.

5) Spread the batter into the prepared pan, and bake for about 40 minutes, or until a knife comes out clean. Cool for 10 minutes, then invert onto a plate. Allow to cool completely before adding the Orange Glaze (same method as on page 11) and / or slicing.

Pound Cake

Preparation time:
15 minutes

Baking time: 50
to 60 minutes

Yield:
12 to 16
servings

   The most basic cake – and the most buttery. Try it plain for
dessert, or topped with fresh Fruit Salad for a serious snack.
You can also slice it thinly and toast it for tea or brunch. A
few variations appear next, and you can explore even further
with your own ideas.

butter and flour for the pan
1 lb. (4 sticks) butter, softened
3 cups sugar
6 eggs

4 cups flour
1 Tbs baking powder
½ tsp. salt
1 cup milk
2 tsp. vanilla extract

1) Preheat oven to 350°F. Butter and flour the bottom and sides of a 10-inch tube or bundt pan.

2) In a large bowl, cream together butter and sugar with an electric mixer at high speed until light and fluffy.

3) Add eggs, one at a time, beating well after each. Set aside.

4) Sift together the dry ingredients in a separate bowl. Mix together the milk and vanilla. Add dry and wet mixtures alternately to butter mixture, beginning and ending with dry. Mix by hand — just enough to blend thoroughly without excess beating.

5) Spread the batter into the prepared pan. Bake 50 to 60 minutes, or until a sharp knife inserted all the way down comes out clean. Allow to cool for 10 minutes in the pan, then turn out onto a plate. Allow to cool completely before slicing.

Pound Cake Variations

Here are some delightful adulterations you can perform in your own kitchen. For each of these variations, follow the pound cake recipe on the previous page, with the following changes:

Lemon Pound Cake

1) Replace vanilla with lemon extract.

2) Add ¼ cup fresh lemon juice.

3) Add 1 tsp. freshly grated lemon rind.

Blueberry Pound Cake

~ Same changes as for Lemon Pound Cake,

plus:

2 cups fresh blueberries, folded in gently with the last addition of dry ingredients

Mocha-Swirl Pound Cake

1) Replace the milk with <u>1 cup strong black coffee</u>.

2) After the batter is all assembled, transfer about ⅓ of it to a small bowl, and add <u>1 oz. (1 square) melted unsweetened chocolate</u>. Mix thoroughly.

3) Spread the plain batter into the prepared pan and spoon clumps of chocolate batter on top. Using a humble dinner knife, cut through to the bottom of the pan and swirl the dark and light together to create a marbled effect. Bake as directed.

Iced Carob Brownies

10 minutes to make
25 minutes to bake

Yield: about
8 servings

If you think of carob as itself and not as a chocolate substitute, you'll appreciate these lovely brownies even more than you would anyway.

butter or margarine for the pan
½ cup (1 stick) melted butter or margarine
¼ cup carob powder
2 eggs
½ cup (packed) light brown sugar
1 tsp. vanilla extract
¼ cup water
1 cup flour
1 tsp. baking powder
¼ tsp. salt
½ cup raisins or currants
½ cup finely chopped walnuts
optional: a dash or two of cinnamon and/or allspice

1) Preheat oven to 350°F. Butter an 8-inch square pan.

2) Beat together butter, carob, eggs, sugar, and vanilla in a medium-sized bowl. Stir in the water.

3) Sift together flour, baking powder, and salt. Stir this into the first mixture along with raisins, nuts, and optional spices. Mix just enough to blend thoroughly.

4) Spread into the prepared pan, and bake 20 to 25 minutes, or until a probe comes out clean. Cool completely before icing.

. . . .

ICING: ¼ cup carob powder
           8 oz. (1 package) cream cheese, softened
           ¼ cup powdered sugar
           ½ tsp. vanilla

Beat everything together until very smooth. Spread on
top of the cooled brownies.

Carrot Cake

❀ ❀ ❀ ❀   ❀ ❀ ❀ ❀

20 minutes to prepare
35 or 40 to 50 minutes to bake

Yield: about 12
to 16 servings

butter, margarine, or oil for the pan(s)
optional: about ¼ cup poppy seeds

1½ cups (3 sticks) butter or margarine, softened
1¾ cups (packed) brown sugar
4 eggs
3 tsp. vanilla extract
1 tsp. grated lemon rind
4 cups flour
1 tsp. salt
½ tsp. baking soda
1 Tbs. baking powder
1 tsp. allspice
2 tsp. cinnamon

2½ cups (packed) finely shredded carrot } combined
¼ cup lemon juice

OPTIONAL ADDITIONS: ¾ cup raisins or currants
¾ cup chopped pecans or walnuts
½ cup shredded unsweetened coconut

1) Preheat oven to 350°F. Generously grease 2 standard-sized loaf pans or 1 oblong pan (9 x 13, or 10 x 14). Sprinkle in the poppy seeds; tilt and shake the pan(s) to distribute the seeds. They will stick nicely.

2) Beat together butter or margarine and sugar in a large bowl. Add eggs, one at a time, beating well after each. When the mixture is fluffy, stir in the vanilla and lemon rind.

3) Sift together the dry ingredients. Add this to the butter mixture alternately with the carrots, beginning and ending with the dry mixture. Mix just enough after each addition to combine — don't overmix. Stir in the optional items (or not) with the last flour addition.

4) Spread the batter evenly in the pan(s), and bake 40 to 50 minutes (loaf pans) or 35 minutes (oblong pan) — or until a probe inserted into the center comes out clean. For loaf pans: cool 10 minutes in the pan, then rap the pan sharply, and dislodge and remove the cake. Transfer to a rack, and let it cool at least 1 hour before slicing.

Banana Bread

20 minutes to prepare
35 or 40 to 50 minutes to bake

Yield: about 12
to 16 servings

    Banana Bread is basically the same recipe as Carrot Cake (page 21), but with the following changes:

1) Replace the poppy seeds with sesame seeds.

2) Use 2½ tsp. vanilla extract and ½ tsp. almond extract.

3) Use orange rind, instead of lemon.

4) Substitute ½ tsp. nutmeg for the allspice.

5) Replace the carrot with 2 cups puréed ripe banana soaked in 1 cup strong black coffee (can be decaf).

6) Omit the raisin/currant and coconut options.

Яussian Coffeecake

30 minutes to prepare
up to 55 minutes to bake

Yield: 1 large cake
(enough for 10 to 12)

a little butter or oil for the pan
1 cup (2 sticks) butter, softened
1 cup (packed) light brown sugar
4 eggs
1 tsp. vanilla extract
2 cups unbleached white flour
1 cup whole wheat pastry flour
1 Tbs. baking powder
1 tsp. baking soda
½ tsp. salt
1 cup buttermilk, at room temperature

```
F ⎧  ½ cup semisweet chocolate chips
I ⎪  ½ cup almonds
L ⎨  ½ cup shredded unsweetened coconut
L ⎪  ½ cup peach or apricot jam
I ⎪  ½ cup dried apricots, minced
N ⎩
G
```

1) Preheat oven to 350°F. Generously grease a standard-size tube or bundt pan.

2) Place the butter and sugar in a large mixing bowl. Cream together with an electric mixer until light and fluffy. Add the eggs one at a time, beating well after each. Stir in the vanilla.

3) Sift together the flours, baking powder, baking soda, and salt into a separate medium-sized bowl.

4) Add the dry mixture and the buttermilk alternately to the butter mixture (dry/wet/dry/wet/dry). Mix just enough to thoroughly blend after each addition. Don't beat or otherwise overmix.

5) Place the chocolate chips and almonds in a blender jar. Whirl together in short spurts until ground into a coarse powder. Combine this with the coconut in a small bowl.

6) Spoon half the batter into the prepared pan, gently spreading it until even. Spoon small amounts of jam here and there onto the batter. (Don't try to spread it—just leave it in little blobs.) Sprinkle on the apricots and about 2/3 of the chocolate-nut mix.

7) Add the remaining batter, distributing it nicely. Sprinkle with the rest of the chocolate mix, and bake the cake for 45 to 55 minutes—until a probing knife inserted all the way in comes out clean. Allow to cool completely before removing from the pan.

Apricot-Almond Bread

40 minutes to prepare
about 1½ hours to bake

Yield: 1 large loaf

Moist and tart with apricots and crunchy with almonds, this bread is ideal for brunches and teas. It's also good as a mid-evening semi-dessert, when you want <u>Something</u> — sweet, but not too — and you don't know exactly what. Try this bread at such times.

butter for the pan
1½ cups thinly sliced
   dried apricots
1½ cups water
2½ cups flour
1 tsp. baking soda
2 tsp. baking powder

1 tsp. salt
2 Tbs. softened butter
½ cup honey or real maple syrup
1 egg, beaten
1 tsp. vanilla extract
½ to 1 tsp. orange rind
1 cup finely chopped almonds

1) Preheat oven to 350°F. Butter a large loaf pan.

2) Place apricots and water in a medium-sized saucepan and bring to a boil. Lower the heat, cover, and simmer for 10 minutes. Transfer to a medium-sized bowl, and allow to cool for about 15 minutes.

3) Sift together dry ingredients (except almonds) in a separate bowl.

4) Stir the butter plus honey or syrup into the cooled apricot mixture. Beat in the egg and vanilla.

5) Add the dry ingredients, orange rind, and almonds. Mix minimally but well.

6) Spread into the prepared pan, and bake about 1½ hours, or until a probe inserted all the way down comes out clean. Let cool for 10 minutes in the pan, then rap the pan firmly a few times on its sides and bottom. The bread should slip right out. Cool at least 15 minutes more before attempting to slice.

Cardamom Coffee Cake

Very rich ~ very delicious

1³/₄ hours
to prepare
and bake

16 servings

oil or butter for the pan
1 lb. (4 sticks) butter or margarine
(or a combination), softened
2 cups (packed) light brown sugar
4 eggs
2 tsp. vanilla extract
4 cups flour
2 tsp. baking powder
2¹/₂ tsp. baking soda

¹/₂ tsp. salt
1 Tbs. powdered cardamom
2 cups sour cream, yogurt,
or buttermilk

NUT MIXTURE:
¹/₄ cup (packed) light brown
sugar
1 Tbs. cinnamon
¹/₂ cup finely chopped
walnuts

1) Preheat oven to 350°F. Butter or oil a 10-inch tube or bundt pan.

2) In a large mixing bowl, beat butter or margarine with sugar until light and fluffy. Add eggs, one at a time, beating well after each. Stir in the vanilla.

3) Sift together the dry ingredients (not including nut mixture ingredients) in a separate bowl.

4) Add the flour mixture, 1/3 of it at a time, to the butter mixture, alternating with the sour cream (or yogurt or buttermilk). Stir just enough to blend after each addition. Don't beat or otherwise overmix.

5) Combine the nut mixture ingredients in a separate bowl.

6) Spoon approximately 1/3 the batter into the prepared pan. Sprinkle with half the nut mixture, then add another third of the batter. Cover with remaining nut mixture, then top with remaining batter. Lightly spread into place.

7) Bake approximately 1 1/4 hours or until a knife inserted all the way in comes out clean. Allow to cool in the pan for 20 minutes, then invert onto a plate. Cool at least 30 minutes more before wildly devouring.

old-fashioned
<u>BREAD</u> <u>PUDDING</u>

10 minutes to prepare
35 minutes to bake

Yield: 6 to 8 servings

   Humble and easy, yet very rewarding. And transcendent served warm, with ice cream!

   This is one of the few instances where ordinary white bread is actually preferable to whole grain.

   3 to 4 packed cups cubed bread
     (OK if stale or frozen)
   3 eggs
   3 cups milk (lowfat OK)
   ⅓ cup sugar (more or less, to taste)
   ½ tsp. salt
   2 tsp. vanilla extract

OPTIONAL TOPPINGS:
{
ice cream
Strawberry-Marmalade Sauce (p.97)
sliced fresh peaches and/or strawberries
}

1) Preheat oven to 350°F. Have ready a 9 x 13-inch baking pan.
2) Spread the bread in the pan.
3) Beat together remaining ingredients. Pour this custard over the bread.
4) Bake about 35 minutes, or until firm but not dry. Serve warm or at room temperature.

VARIATIONS

POOR PERSON'S TRIFLE

add to custard
- ¼ cup rum
- 1½ cups crushed pineapple au jus (canned-in-juice = fine)
- 1½ cups berries or pitted cherries (frozen unsweetened = fine. No need to defrost.)

OPTIONAL: 1 cup chopped walnuts

BREAD & CHOCOLATE PUDDING

Add to the bread: 1½ cups semisweet chocolate chips

BANANA BREAD PUDDING

Add to the bread: 1 or 2 ripe bananas, sliced.

OPTIONAL: a few dashes of cinnamon and nutmeg.

STRAWBERRY-RHUBARB CRISP

Preparation time: 15 minutes

Baking time: 35 to 40 minutes

Yield: about 6 servings

...An easy cobbler with a very crunchy top. Use the smaller amount of sugar if you like it tart. It would be a good idea to have some vanilla ice cream on hand, since you might decide that you can't bear not to have this dessert à la mode.

2 lbs. fresh rhubarb,
  cut into 1-inch chunks
3 to 4 cups sliced strawberries
1/3 to 1/2 cup white sugar
1 1/4 cups rolled oats
1 cup flour

1/4 cup brown sugar
3/4 tsp. cinnamon
a dash or two of both
  allspice and nutmeg
1/2 tsp. salt
1/2 cup (1 stick) melted butter

1) Preheat oven to 375°F.

2) Combine the rhubarb and strawberries in a 9-inch square pan. Sprinkle with white sugar.

3) Mix together the remaining ingredients in a medium-sized bowl. Distribute over the top of the fruit and pat firmly into place.

4) Bake uncovered for 35 to 40 minutes, or until the top is crisp and lightly browned and the fruit is bubbling around the edges. Serve hot, warm, or at room temperature, plain or à la mode.

variations using other fruits:
APPLE CRISP
- Use 6 to 8 cups peeled and sliced tart apples
- 2 to 3 Tbs. lemon juice
- ¼ cup white sugar
- increase cinnamon (use up to 1 tsp.)
- optional: add ½ cup finely chopped walnuts to the topping

PEACH (or APRICOT) - CHERRY CRISP
- Use about 4 cups peeled and sliced peaches or apricots, plus 2 cups pitted, halved dark cherries (OK to use frozen unsweetened)
- Same adjustments as in Apple Crisp. In addition, you can increase the nutmeg to ¼ tsp. and use almonds instead of walnuts in the topping.

Peach Puddingcake

20 minutes to prepare
30 minutes to bake

Yield: one
9 x 13-inch cake

a little butter or oil for the pan
2 cups unbleached white flour
2 tsp. baking powder
½ tsp. salt
1 tsp. cinnamon
½ tsp. allspice
2 eggs

1 cup (packed) light brown sugar
1 cup milk (lowfat or soy ok)
1 tsp. vanilla extract
¼ tsp. almond extract
2 Tbs. melted butter
2½ cups sliced peaches (fresh
    or frozen/defrosted)

TOPPING:
{
½ pint heavy cream, whipped, or
1 cup firm yogurt
2 Tbs. rum (optional)
maple syrup to taste
}

1) Preheat oven to 350°F. Lightly grease a 9 x 13-inch baking pan.

2) Sift flour, baking powder, salt, and spices into a medium-sized bowl.

3) In a separate bowl, beat together the eggs and brown sugar with an electric mixer at high speed for about 2 minutes. Stir in the milk, extracts, and melted butter.

4) Make a well in the center of the dry ingredients, and pour in the wet. Add the peaches, and stir with a wooden spoon until well combined.

5) Spread into the prepared pan and bake for about 30 minutes, or until a toothpick inserted all the way into the center comes out clean.

6) In a small bowl, fold together the whipped cream or yogurt with rum, if desired, and maple syrup to taste. Serve the puddingcake at any temperature, with a generous amount of topping.

Peach Twig, early June

Spicy Gingerbread

20 minutes
to prepare
30 to 35 minutes
to bake

Yield:
6 to 9 servings

a little butter or oil for the pan
6 Tbs. butter or canola oil
3 Tbs. grated fresh ginger
1/2 cup light-colored honey
1/2 cup light molasses
3/4 cup firm yogurt
1 egg
2 cups unbleached white flour
1 1/2 tsp. baking soda
1/4 tsp. salt
1 tsp. dry mustard
1/2 tsp. ground cloves or allspice
1/2 tsp. cinnamon
1/4 tsp. nutmeg

1) Preheat oven to 350°F. Grease an 8-inch square pan (or its equivalent).

2) Melt the butter or heat the oil in a small skillet. Add the ginger, and sauté together over medium heat for about 3 minutes, or until fragrant. Remove from heat.

3) Combine honey and molasses in a small mixing bowl, and beat at high speed with an electric mixer for 2 to 3 minutes. Add the ginger mixture, and beat for a minute more. Whisk in the yogurt and egg, then beat at high speed for an additional minute. Set aside.

4) Sift the dry ingredients together into a large mixing bowl. Make a well in the center, and pour in the wet mixture. Mix with a few decisive strokes until thoroughly combined.

5) Spread into the prepared pan. Bake 30 to 35 minutes, or until the top surface is springy to the touch. Cool at least 15 minutes before slicing.

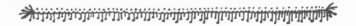

LEMON MOUSSE

1 hour to prepare
plus time to chill

Yield:
6 servings

Ethereal, yet it packs a tangy punch. Serve Lemon Mousse by itself or topped with Strawberry-Marmalade Sauce (p. 97). It also goes beautifully served in tandem with many different cakes, especially Ukrainian Poppy Seed Cake (p. 13).

Lemon Mousse will keep well for several days if tightly covered and refrigerated.

¼ cup cornstarch
½ cup sugar
½ cup freshly squeezed lemon juice
½ cup water
1 tsp. grated lemon rind
2 egg whites, at room temperature
½ pint heavy cream

OPTIONAL VARIATIONS:
1 cup berries or sliced peaches
orange rind, instead of lemon

1) Place cornstarch and sugar in a small saucepan. Add lemon juice and water and whisk until smooth.

2) Cook, whisking constantly, over medium heat until thick (5 to 8 minutes). Remove from heat, transfer to a medium-sized bowl, and stir in the lemon rind. Let cool to room temperature.

3) Place the egg whites in a medium-sized mixing bowl and beat at high speed with an electric mixer until stiff but not dry. Fold this into the lemon mixture, cover tightly, and chill at least 1 hour (longer = also OK).

4) Without cleaning the beaters, whip the cream until it is firm but still fluffy. Fold this into the mousse (add optional berries or peaches at this point), cover tightly again, and chill until serving time.

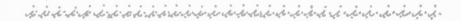

Fresh Strawberry Mousse

NEW! NO EGGS!
DELICIOUS NONFAT OPTION!

Preparation time:
20 minutes of doing things,
plus time to cool and chill

Yield:
4 to 6
servings

4 cups sliced strawberries
6 Tbs. cornstarch
2/3 cup sugar
1/2 cup fresh lemon juice
1 tsp. grated lemon rind

1/2 pint heavy cream, whipped
OR
1 cup firm yogurt (nonfat OK),
stirred until smooth

1) Place the strawberries in a medium-sized saucepan. Cover and cook over medium heat for 5 to 8 minutes, until it looks like soup. Transfer to a medium-sized bowl and set aside.

2) Without washing it first, use the same saucepan for this step. Combine the cornstarch, sugar, and lemon juice in the pan, and whisk until uniform.

3) Pour the still-hot strawberry soup back into the cornstarch mixture, whisking constantly. Return the pan to the stove, and cook over medium heat, stirring constantly until thick. (This should take about 5 minutes.) Remove from heat, and stir in the lemon rind.

4) Transfer back to the same bowl the strawberries had been in, and cool to room temperature.

5) Purée until smooth in a food processor or blender, and return to the bowl. Cover tightly and chill until cold.

6) Fold in the whipped cream or yogurt and serve.

🍎 Apple Strudel 🍎

30 minutes to prepare
35 minutes to bake

Yield:
8 to 10 servings

This delicious and straightforward Apple Strudel can be made several days in advance and stored, unbaked, in the refrigerator (tightly wrapped). Baked Strudel also keeps very well in the refrigerator or freezer if wrapped airtight. If you freeze it, defrost it completely before reheating it, uncovered, in a 350°F oven for about 20 minutes — or until crispened.

NOTE: To make fine bread crumbs, cut several thick slices of whole wheat or white bread, and let them dry out for a few hours. Then toast the slices lightly, and grind them to a fine meal in a blender or a food processor.

6 Tbs. vegetable oil – OR ½ cup melted butter – OR oil spray

1½ lbs. tart apples (about 8 medium ones), peeled and chopped

¼ cup sugar

A pinch of salt

1 tsp. cinnamon

3 Tbs. fresh lemon juice

1 Tbs. grated lemon rind

½ cup minced walnuts, lightly toasted

½ cup fine bread crumbs

¼ cup raisins (optional)

1 cup grated cheddar (optional)

A 1-lb. package filo pastry

1) Preheat oven to 375°F. Brush a baking tray with a little of the oil or melted butter, or spray it with oil spray. (Save most of the oil or butter for the filo.)

2) Place all the ingredients except the filo in a large bowl, and toss gently until everything is evenly distributed.

3) Place a sheet of filo on a clean, dry surface, and brush it lightly all over with oil or melted butter — or spray it with oil spray. Lay another sheet on top, oil or butter it all over, and continue until you have a pile of 6. Distribute ⅓ of the apple mixture here,

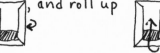

fold over the sides, and roll up this way.

4) Oil or butter the top of the roll, then transfer it to the prepared tray. Repeat with the remaining ingredients to make 2 more rolls.

5) Bake for about 35 minutes, or until lightly browned and exquisitely crisp. Serve warm or at room temperature.

CHOCOLATE MERINGUES

10 minutes to prepare
3 hours to bake

Yield: 1½ dozen
(easily doubled)

Meringues have the great ability to satisfy all longings for a rich dessert, yet they contain no butter, oil, egg yolks, or flour.

These two versions provide a contrast of textures: an ethereal crunch on the first bite, followed by full-bodied chewiness. The baking process is slow and gradual — almost more of a drying-out than an actual baking.

1 cup powdered sugar
2 Tbs. cocoa
a pinch of salt
OPTIONAL:
¼ cup hazelnuts,
    pecans, or almonds

4 egg whites
½ tsp. vanilla
optional: ½ cup
    chocolate chips

1) Preheat oven to 250°F. Lightly grease a baking tray - OR line it with parchment or waxed paper.

2) Sift together powdered sugar, cocoa, and salt. If you're adding nuts, place them in a blender or food processor with the sugar mixture, and grind in a series of spurts until the nuts and sugar form a fine powder.

3) Beat together the egg whites and vanilla at high speed until they form stiff peaks. Fold in the sugar-nut mixture (or just the cocoa-sugar) and the chocolate chips.

4) Drop by rounded tablespoonfuls onto the prepared tray.

5) Bake the meringues for 2½ to 3 hours without opening the oven. Then turn off the oven, and leave them in there for at least 15 minutes. (You can also leave them in for up to an hour or two. This part is flexible!) Cool completely before removing them from the tray.

NOTE: Meringues will turn out softer or firmer, depending on the humidity in your kitchen. Store them in an airtight bin lined with waxed paper.

ONE MORE THING: Separate the eggs while they're cold, then let the whites come to room temperature.

45

Fruited Yogurt Desserts

Almost any combination of fruit and yogurt will taste delicious - and make a filling lowfat dessert. Here are a few suggestions. Combine as close to serving time as possible.

I.

3 cups plain yogurt
1 cup fresh blueberries
1 cup seedless grapes
1 cup pitted, halved cherries
sugar, maple syrup, or honey
~to taste

Combine and chill.

II.

3 cups plain yogurt
1 cup fresh strawberries, halved
1 to 2 medium-sized ripe
peaches, sliced
1 perfectly ripe banana, sliced
sugar, honey, or maple syrup
~to taste

Combine and chill.

III.

3 cups plain yogurt
1 to 2 medium-sized apples,
grated
½ cup lightly toasted minced
almonds
a dash of cinnamon
sugar, maple syrup, or honey
~to taste

Combine and chill.

Apple

Custard

Pie

Preparation time: 25 minutes   **Yield:** 4 to 6 servings
Baking time: 45 minutes

2 cups peeled and thinly sliced tart apples
1 unbaked 9-inch pie crust (p.61)
4 eggs (ok to omit 2 of the yolks)
¼ to ⅓ cup brown sugar or honey
1 cup yogurt
1 tsp. vanilla extract
½ tsp. cinnamon
¼ tsp. salt

1) Preheat oven to 375°F.

2) Spread the apple slices evenly over the unbaked pie crust.

3) Combine all remaining ingredients in a food processor or blender and whip until frothy. Pour this custard over the apples.

4) Bake for 45 minutes, or until solid in the center. Cool for at least 1 hour before slicing. This pie tastes best at room temperature or cold.

No-Fault Pumpkin Pie

20 minutes to prepare
50 minutes to bake
(including crust)

Yield: 1 compact
9-inch pie (about
6 to 8 servings)

2 cups cooked, puréed pumpkin or squash
  (Canned pumpkin is fine)
1/4 cup white sugar
1/4 cup brown sugar
2 Tbs. molasses
1/2 tsp. ground cloves or allspice
2 tsp. cinnamon
2 tsp. powdered ginger
3/4 tsp. salt
2 beaten eggs
1 cup evaporated milk (lowfat ok)
1 unbaked 9-inch pie crust (p.61)

OPTIONAL TOPPINGS:
whipped cream with a little sugar and rum
whipped cream with a little sugar and vanilla extract
vanilla ice cream

1) Preheat oven to 375°F.

2) Place pumpkin or squash purée in a medium-sized bowl, and add all other filling ingredients. Beat until smooth.

3) Spread into the pie crust and bake at 375° for 10 minutes. Turn the oven down to 350°, and bake another 40 minutes, or until the pie is firm in the center when shaken lightly.

4) Cool at least to room temperature before serving. This pie tastes very good chilled, with rum- or vanilla-spiked whipped cream, or some high-quality vanilla ice cream.

Maple-Walnut Pie

Delicious — and very easy!

Preparation time:
20 minutes

Baking time:
30 minutes

Yield:
about 6
servings

4 large eggs
¾ cup real maple syrup
2 Tbs. lemon juice
¼ to ½ tsp. cinnamon (to taste)
1½ tsp. vanilla extract
¼ tsp. salt
2 cups chopped walnuts
1 unbaked 9-inch pie crust (p. 61)
OPTIONAL: whipped cream, for the top

1) Preheat oven to 375°F.

2) Beat together all ingredients, except walnuts and pie crust, until light and frothy.

3) Spread the walnuts into the unbaked crust. Pour in the batter.

4) Bake for 30 minutes or until solid in the center. Remove from oven and allow to cool for at least 30 minutes before serving.

5) Serve warm, at room temperature, or cold, with or without whipped cream.

Crunchy-Top Peach Pie

Preparation time: about 40 minutes   Yield: 6 servings
Baking time: about another 40 minutes

Make this at the height of peach season, with the finest, ripest peaches available. Or, you can freeze some of those same fine, ripe peaches (peel and slice them first; spread on a tray and freeze, then transfer to a plastic bag, seal, and store in the freezer), and surprise everyone with this delightful pie in November.

If you have access to some equally fine and ripe apricots, they will work equally well.

6 cups sliced ripe peaches
1/4 to 1/3 cup sugar
3 Tbs. fresh lemon juice
3 Tbs. flour
1 tsp. cinnamon
a few dashes of nutmeg
1 unbaked 9-inch pie crust (p.61)

TOPPING:
2 cups rolled oats
1/4 cup flour
1/2 tsp. salt
1/2 tsp. cinnamon
1/2 cup minced almonds
3 Tbs. brown sugar
5 Tbs. melted butter

POSSIBLE ACCOMPANIMENTS:
ice cream (recommended: vanilla, almond, or amaretto)
whipped cream
nothing at all

1) Preheat oven to 400°F.

2) Place peaches in a medium-sized bowl and sprinkle with sugar and lemon juice.

3) Combine 3 Tbs. flour and spices, and sprinkle this into the peaches. Mix gently but thoroughly. Spread this filling into the unbaked crust.

4) Combine topping ingredients in the same bowl (no need to wash it first), and mix well. Apply the topping evenly over the top, patting it firmly into place.

5) Bake for 10 minutes at 400°F, then turn the oven down to 375° and bake for about 30 minutes more. Serve warm or cold, with ice cream or whipped cream, or just plain.

Apple~Port~Cheese Pie
with Almond Crust

Preparation time:
CRUST = 40 minutes
APPLES = 20 minutes
FILLING = 10 minutes
GLAZE + ASSEMBLY = 10 minutes

Yield:
about 6
servings

At first glance, this scrumptious cheese-filled, apple-glazed, almond-crusted pie seems like a lot of work, but it's really quite easy. I've broken down the tasks in the "preparation time" posted above, and everything but the glaze and assembly can be done in advance.

So go ahead and try this. You'll love it so much, you'll want to make it again tomorrow.

I. THE CRUST:

½ cup (1 stick) cold butter
1 cup unbleached white flour (plus extra for rolling out)
¼ cup ground almonds
3 to 4 Tbs. cold water
(foil and 2 cups dry beans for the baking)

1) Preheat oven to 375°F.

2) Use a pastry cutter or food processor to cut together the butter and flour until the mixture has the texture of coarse cornmeal. Stir in the almonds.

3) Sprinkle in the water as needed, mixing quickly with a fork or a few additional spurts of the food processor, until a firm, cohesive dough is formed.

4) Flour a rolling pin and a clean, dry surface, and roll the dough into a circle large enough to fit a 9-inch pie or tart pan. Ease the dough into the pan, pat it into place, and use your hands to form a nice edge.

5) Pierce the crust all over with a fork. Cut a piece of foil approximately to fit, and place this on top of the crust. Sprinkle about 2 cups dry beans over the foil (this keeps it flat during baking) and bake 15 minutes. Remove the foil and beans, and bake 15 minutes more. Cool before filling. (You can turn off the oven — the rest of the pie is unbaked.)

II. THE APPLES & PORT:

1½ cups port (or a comparable
    sweet dessert wine)
1 stick cinnamon
½ tsp. grated lemon rind

3 large (3-inch diameter)
    tart apples, peeled
    and sliced thin
⅓ cup light-colored honey
a dash of salt

1) Combine port, cinnamon stick, lemon rind, and apples in a
medium-sized saucepan. Bring to a boil, turn heat down to low,
cover, and simmer for 10 minutes — or until the apples are
perfectly tender. Remove from heat and discard the cinnamon stick.

2) Strain, reserving both the apples and the liquid. Stir the honey
and salt into the liquid. Set aside.

III. THE CHEESE FILLING:

6 oz. (¾ cup) cream cheese, softened
½ tsp. vanilla extract
¼ tsp. almond extract
2 Tbs. light-colored honey
¼ cup firm yogurt

1) Combine all ingredients in a small mixing bowl, and beat until smooth. Spread evenly into the baked, cooled crust.

2) Arrange the cooked apple slices on top in a lovely pattern.

IV. THE GLAZE:

    2 Tbs. cornstarch
    1½ cups of the apple-cooking liquid

1) Place the cornstarch in a small saucepan. Whisk in the liquid, and keep whisking as you bring the mixture to a boil. Turn the heat down, and cook, stirring frequently, until thick and glossy (approximately 5 to 8 minutes).

2) Without waiting for it to cool, pour the glaze over the lovely pattern of apples. Cool to room temperature, then chill until cold.

Cherry-Berry Pie

20 minutes to make the crust
10 minutes to make the filling
45 to 50 minutes to bake

Yield:
4 to 6
servings

NOTE: You can use frozen unsweetened fruit.
Defrost and drain before using.

I. THE CRUST:

2 cups unbleached white flour

1/4 teaspoon salt

3/4 cup (1 1/2 sticks) cold unsalted butter

4 to 6 Tbs. cold milk

Extra flour, as needed, for rolling the dough

1) Place the flour and salt in a food processor fitted with the steel blade attachment.

2) Cut the butter into slices and drop them on top of the flour.

3) Pulse until the flour and butter are combined, and the mixture resembles a coarse meal. (You shouldn't see any big pieces of butter at this point.)

4) Add milk, 1 tablespoon at a time, pulsing after each addition. When the dough sticks to itself when gently squeezed, dump it out onto a clean, dry surface. Use your hands to press it into two balls, one larger and one smaller.

5) Using flour, as needed, to prevent sticking, roll the larger ball to fit a 9- or 10-inch pie pan. Roll the smaller ball of dough, as well, and cut it into about 12 ½-inch strips. Refrigerate until ready to use.

II. THE FILLING:

3 cups berries ~ any kind
   (Slice larger ones;
   leave smaller ones whole)
3 cups dark cherries, pitted
3/4 cup sugar
1 tsp. grated lemon rind
1/2 tsp. cinnamon
About 3 grates fresh nutmeg
2 Tbs. fresh lemon juice
6 Tbs. unbleached white flour
A pinch of salt
Confectioners' sugar for the top (optional)

1) Preheat oven to 375°F.

2) Gently toss together all the ingredients (except the confectioners' sugar) in a large bowl. When the filling is uniformly mixed, spoon it into the unbaked crust.

3) Decorate the top with the strips of dough, either in a woven pattern (a lattice), or just by laying the strips on top, and possibly twisting them a little. It will look beautiful, whatever you do. Press the ends of the strips to the edges of the crust.

4) Place the pie pan on a baking tray, and place the tray in the lower half of the oven. Bake for 45 to 50 minutes, or until bubbly and lightly browned. Serve warm, at room temperature, or cold, with confectioners' sugar dusted on top, if desired.

Chocolate Crêpes

Preparation time:
Making the crêpes – 30 minutes
Filling them – 15 minutes

Yield:
8 crêpes
(4 servings)

It might sound complicated, but this recipe is actually very simple.

The crêpes can be made up to several days in advance and stored on a plate, tightly wrapped and refrigerated.

Heating and filling the crêpes – and getting them ready to serve – takes practically no time at all. The only challenge involved is to eat them slowly. It's almost impossible not to wolf them down!

I. Making the Crêpes:

1 egg
½ cup plus 2 Tbs. milk
a dash of salt
½ cup unbleached white flour
1 Tbs. unsweetened cocoa
2 Tbs. sugar
a little oil for the pan

1) Combine everything but the oil in a blender and whip until smooth.

2) Use a 6- or 7-inch crêpe or omelette pan — nonstick, if possible. Heat the pan, and brush lightly with oil.

3) Keep the heat high, and add just enough batter to coat the pan (about 2 or 3 Tbs. batter). Tilt the pan every which way until it is fairly evenly coated. Wait a few seconds for the crêpe to set.

4) Loosen the sides and flip it over. Cook on this side for about 10 seconds, then turn out the finished crêpe onto a dinner plate.

5) Continue making crêpes until you have used up the batter. (Don't forget to keep the heat high throughout the cooking.) Stack the crêpes on the dinner plate. Cover tightly with plastic wrap, and refrigerate until you're ready to fill them.

Filling and Serving the Crêpes:

a little butter for the pan
1 cup orange marmalade OR
   1 cup semisweet chocolate chips
1/2 cup heavy cream (possibly more)
Confectioners' sugar ⎫
unsweetened cocoa ⎭ for the top

1) Heat a large skillet or a sauté pan over medium heat. When it is hot, add some butter, and push or swirl it all around until it melts and the pan is coated.

2) Add a crêpe, and let it heat on one side for about a minute. Then turn it over, and add about 2 Tbs. orange marmalade or chocolate chips to the center. Spread the filling around a little.

3) Fold the crêpe like so:

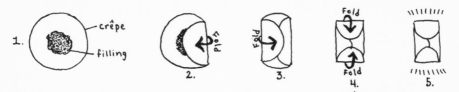

1. crêpe / filling

4) Push the filled, folded crêpe to the side of the pan, add a little more butter, and proceed with the next crêpe. (If the pan gets too crowded with filled crêpes, you can move some to a second warmed, buttered pan.)

5) To serve, put about a tablespoon of cream on each serving plate, and swirl it around. Place one or two warmed crêpes on top, and dust lightly with confectioners' sugar and unsweetened cocoa. Serve right away.

Stuffed Baked Apples

* * * * * * * * * * * * * * *

1 hour to prepare (including 40 minutes of baking)

Put these in the oven as you sit down to dinner.
They'll be ready just in time to eat hot for dessert.

Yield: 6 servings
NOTE: If you have leftover filling, sprinkle it on top
at serving time.

Good for breakfast or brunch, as well as dessert.

6 large, tart apples
½ cup Grape Nuts cereal
¼ cup finely minced walnuts or almonds
½ tsp. cinnamon
1 to 2 Tbs. brown sugar
2 cups apple juice
a few strips of fresh lemon peel
1 cinnamon stick

TOPPING
yogurt, sweetened to taste with a little maple syrup

1) Preheat oven to 375°F.

2) Carefully remove the cores from the apples, using an apple corer (highly specialized gadget), a vegetable peeler, an agile paring knife, and/or a teaspoon handle. Try to get all the seeds out of there, as well as anything else you'd prefer not to bite into.

3) Combine cereal, nuts, cinnamon, and sugar in a small bowl.

4) Place the apples in a glass baking pan, and stuff their cavities with the filling. Pour the apple juice around them; float the lemon peel and cinnamon stick in the juice. Cover loosely with foil, and bake for about 40 minutes, or until the apples can be pierced easily with a knife.

5) Serve hot, warm, at room temperature, or cold. Spoon some of the juice over the top, and spoon on some lightly sweetened yogurt.

• • • • • • • • • • • • • • •

✶ Chocolate ✶ Apple ✶ Nut Torte ✶

25 minutes to prepare
45 minutes to bake
plus time to cool

Yield:
6 to 8
servings

NOTES:
1) Separate the eggs ahead of time.
2) Grind almonds & chocolate in a blender or food processor.
3) Use a food processor to grate the apple.

8 eggs (OK to delete half the yolks)
a little butter or oil for the pan
3/4 cup sugar
1 cup almonds, finely ground
1 cup (packed) grated tart apple
3/4 cup semisweet chocolate chips,
   ground to a coarse meal
1/2 cup unbleached white flour *

1/2 tsp. baking powder
   (optional)
dash of cinnamon
1/2 tsp. salt
1/2 tsp. vanilla extract
OPTIONAL TOPPING:
whipped cream laced with
   a little Amaretto liqueur

* Fine bread crumbs or matzo cake meal can replace the flour.

1) (Do this ahead): Separate the eggs, placing both whites and yolks in large mixing bowls. Cover each bowl, and let the eggs come to room temperature.

2) Preheat the oven to 350°F. Grease the bottom only of a 9- or 10-inch spring-form pan.

3) Beat the egg whites until they form stiff peaks. Set aside.

4) Without cleaning the beaters, beat together the egg yolks and sugar for about 2 minutes. Stir in the almonds, apple, and chocolate.

5) Sift the flour, baking powder, cinnamon, and salt directly into the yolk mixture. Add the vanilla, and stir until well combined.

6) Gently fold in the beaten egg whites, using a rubber spatula to scrape the heavier mixture from the bottom of the bowl. Try to incorporate the whites as well as possible without deflating them too much. (This is an imperfect process, so don't worry if the folded batter isn't uniform.) Turn into the prepared pan.

7) Bake for about 45 minutes, or until a toothpick inserted into the center comes out clean. Cool thoroughly before removing the sides of the pan and slicing.

old-fashioned, made-from-scratch

Chocolate ❖ Pudding

15 minutes to prepare
plus about 2 hours
    to chill

Yield:
4 servings

Real! Genuine! The mother of all comfort foods!

GOOD NEWS FOR VEGANS: This tastes absolutely
wonderful made with plain or vanilla soy milk.

3/4 to 1 cup semisweet chocolate chips

2 to 3 Tbs. light brown sugar

2 cups milk (lowfat or soy OK)

a pinch of salt

3 Tbs. cornstarch

1/2 tsp. vanilla extract

1) Combine the chocolate, sugar, and milk in a medium-sized heavy saucepan. Heat gently, whisking constantly, until all the chocolate is melted and the mixture is uniform. Remove from heat.

2) Place the salt and cornstarch in a medium-small bowl. Pour in about half the hot mixture, whisking vigorously until all the cornstarch is dissolved, then whisk this solution back into the saucepan.

3) Keep stirring as you cook the pudding over very low heat for about 8 to 10 minutes more, or until thick and glossy. Remove from heat and stir in the vanilla.

4) Transfer the hot pudding to a serving bowl or to individual cups. To avoid a skin forming on top, lay a sheet of waxed paper over the surface. Chill completely before serving.

DANISH CHERRIES

Preparation time:
about 30 minutes

Yield: about
6 servings

Make this delicious, beautiful, and very simple stovetop dessert well in advance OR right before serving. You can get fine results from frozen cherries (they come pitted and unsweetened in sealed plastic bags), if fresh are unavailable. No need to defrost before using.

NOTES: ♪ To blanch almonds, place them in a colander over a sink. Pour boiling water over them, and rub off the skins. Cut vertically with a sharp knife to sliver them.

♪ To whip ricotta, beat it vigorously with a whisk, or at high speed with an electric mixer.

4 cups pitted cherries
1½ Tbs. cornstarch
3 to 4 Tbs. sugar

¼ cup lemon juice
½ tsp. grated lemon rind
¾ tsp. almond extract

OPTIONAL: ½ cup blanched, slivered almonds

TOPPINGS: whipped cream
         or
    whipped ricotta cheese } with a few blanched, slivered almonds folded in
         or
    plain yogurt

1) Place cherries in a heavy medium-sized saucepan, and cook over medium heat, covered, for 10 minutes.

2) Meanwhile, combine cornstarch and sugar in a small bowl. Add lemon juice and whisk until smooth. Stir this into the hot cherries, and cook over medium heat, stirring frequently, until thick (5 to 8 minutes).

3) Remove from heat and stir in lemon rind, almond extract, and slivered almonds. Serve hot, warm, room temperature, or cold, topped with whipped cream, whipped ricotta, or yogurt.

Baked Custard

Yield: 6 custard cups

Easy super-comfort food

BITTERSWEET CHOCOLATE CUSTARD:

Preparation time: 20 minutes (45 minutes to bake)

2½ cups milk (lowfat works just fine)
¾ to 1 cup semisweet chocolate chips
(depending on how deeply chocophilic you are)
4 eggs
½ tsp. salt
1 tsp. vanilla extract

1) Preheat oven to 350°F. Have ready six ovenproof custard cups and a 9 x 13-inch baking pan.

2) Place the milk and chocolate chips in a small saucepan. Heat gently, stirring occasionally, until all the chips are melted. Remove from heat and stir until blended. Allow to cool for about 15 minutes.

3) Place remaining ingredients in a blender or food processor. Add the milk mixture, scraping in all the wayward clumps of chocolate, and whip until frothy.

4) Divide the batter among the custard cups. Place them in the baking pan, and half-fill it with water. Bake 40 to 45 minutes, or until the custards are solid in the center when shaken.

5) Carefully remove the cups from the baking pan. Cool to room temperature, then cover each one tightly with plastic wrap and chill.

MAPLE CUSTARD
Preparation time: 10 minutes
(45 minutes to bake)

omit chocolate chips
add ¹/₃ cup real maple syrup
optional: a dash each of cinnamon and nutmeg

~ Skip Step 2. Blend all ingredients together in Step 3. Bake as directed.

MAPLE-PEACH CUSTARD

Preparation time: 15 minutes
(45 minutes to bake)

1½ to 2 cups sliced fresh peaches

~ Make Maple Custard batter. Divide the peaches among the custard cups, pour the custard over the peaches, and bake as directed.

Coconut & Almond Macaroon Torte

PREPARATION TIME:
20 minutes to prepare
35 minutes to bake
(plus time to cool
   and a few minutes
   to finish)

Yield:
about 6
servings

6 eggs
a little oil or butter for the pan
1 ⅓ cups almonds, lightly toasted
½ cup sugar
1 cup shredded unsweetened
   coconut, lightly toasted

½ tsp. salt
2 tsp. grated orange rind
½ cup raspberry preserves
¾ cup chocolate chips
fresh raspberries, if
   available, for garnish

1) ABOUT 1 HOUR AHEAD: Separate the eggs, placing the whites in a large bowl and the yolks in a smaller bowl. Cover and let come to room temperature.

2) Lightly grease the bottom of a 9-inch springform pan. Preheat oven to 375°F.

3) Place the almonds in a food processor with 1 tablespoon of the sugar. Use a series of long pulses to grind the almonds to a powder. Transfer to a medium-sized bowl; stir in the coconut, salt, and orange rind, and set aside.

4) Measure out another tablespoon of the sugar, add it to the egg whites, and beat until they form stiff peaks.

5) Add the remaining sugar to the egg yolks, and beat with a fork or a small whisk until the sugar is incorporated. Fold this mixture into the beaten whites.

6) Sprinkle the dry mixture over the beaten, folded eggs, and finish folding. Transfer to the prepared pan, and bake in the center of the oven for about 35 minutes, or until a sharp knife inserted all the way into the center comes out clean. Remove from the oven, and cool completely.

7) When the cake is cool, release the springform sides, and transfer the cake to a plate. Spread the raspberry preserves over the top.

8) Melt the chocolate, and spread it over the preserves. Decorate with fresh raspberries, if available.

Jewish New Year Honeycake

15 to 20 minutes
to assemble
45 minutes to bake

(The apple topping takes
about 20 minutes)

Yield:
6 to 8
servings

a little butter or oil for the pan	a scant ½ tsp. salt
1 cup light-colored honey	2½ tsp. baking powder
1 egg	cinnamon
3 Tbs. canola oil or melted butter	nutmeg } a dash or two of each
½ cup cold black coffee — or water	allspice
2 cups unbleached white flour	½ cup minced walnuts

1) Preheat oven to 350°F. Grease a medium-sized loaf pan.

2) Place the honey in a medium-sized bowl, and beat at high speed with an electric mixer for about 3 minutes.

3) Add the egg, oil or butter, and coffee or water. Beat for 1 more minute.

4) Sift the flour, salt, baking powder, and spices directly into the honey mixture. Add half the walnuts, and stir until well combined.

5) Spread the batter into the prepared pan, and sprinkle the remaining nuts on top.

6) Bake for about 45 minutes, or until a knife inserted all the way into the center comes out clean. Cool in the pan for about 15 minutes, then rap the pan sharply to remove the cake. Cool thoroughly before slicing.

DELICIOUS APPLE TOPPING:

> 4 cups peeled, sliced tart apple
> 1 to 2 Tbs. fresh lemon juice
> 3/4 tsp. cinnamon
> OPTIONAL: honey to taste

1) Place apples, lemon juice, and cinnamon in a medium-sized saucepan. Cover and cook over medium heat until the apples are soft (about 10 minutes).

2) Remove from heat, and stir in honey to taste, if desired.

3) Spoon it, still hot or warm, onto slices of cooled honeycake.

Chocolate Honeycake

25 minutes to prepare
25 minutes to bake
   (square pan)
35 to 40 minutes to bake
   (loaf pan)

Yield:
6 to 8 servings

a little butter or oil for the pan
½ cup butter (1 stick) or canola oil
1 oz. (1 square) unsweetened
   chocolate
¾ cup light-colored honey
2 eggs
1 tsp. vanilla extract

¼ cup unsweetened cocoa
1 cup unbleached white flour
½ tsp. salt
1½ tsp. baking powder
1 cup chocolate chips
½ cup chopped nuts
   (optional)

1) Preheat oven to 350°F. Grease an 8-inch square pan or a medium-sized loaf pan.

2) Melt the butter and chocolate together over low heat. If using oil, melt the chocolate alone, then remove from heat and stir in the oil.

3) Place the honey in a medium-sized bowl, and beat at high speed with an electric mixer for about 2 minutes. Add the eggs one at a time, beating well after each. Stir in the vanilla.

4) Sift together the dry ingredients into a separate medium-small bowl.

5) Beat the melted chocolate mixture into the honey-egg mixture. Fold in the dry ingredients and chocolate chips (and optional nuts), and stir until well combined. Spread into the prepared pan.

6) Bake about 25 minutes (square pan) or 35 to 40 minutes (loaf pan). It's done when a knife inserted all the way into the center comes out clean. Cool before slicing.

❋ ❋ ❋ Carob Fudge Torte ❋ ❋ ❋

....very moist and loveable.

I. Cake

30 minutes to prepare
30 minutes to bake
(plus time to cool
and assemble)

Yield: a big
layer cake
(enough to serve
10 to 12)

a little butter or oil for the pans

½ cup butter (1 stick), softened

¾ cup light-colored honey

2 eggs

½ cup carob powder

½ cup hot water or coffee

2 cups unbleached white flour

1 tsp. baking soda

½ tsp. salt

1 cup firm yogurt

1½ tsp. vanilla extract

1) Preheat oven to 350°F. Grease 2 8-inch round cake pans.

2) Place the butter and honey in a large mixing bowl. Cream together, using an electric mixer at high speed, for 3 minutes.

3) Add the eggs one at a time, beating well after each.

4) Combine the carob powder and hot water or coffee in a small bowl. Mix until it becomes a smooth paste, then beat this into the butter mixture until uniformly blended.

5) Sift together the dry ingredients into a separate medium-sized bowl. Stir this mixture into the carob-butter mixture alternately with the yogurt (flour / yogurt / flour / yogurt / flour). With each addition, mix just enough to combine. (Overmixing will toughen the cake's texture.) Stir in vanilla.

6) Divide the batter evenly between the cake pans. Bake for 20 to 30 minutes, or until a toothpick inserted into the center comes out clean.

7) Cool in the pans for 10 minutes, then remove by rapping the pans sharply and inverting the cakes onto dinner plates. Cool thoroughly.

II. Orange-Cream Cheese Frosting

8 oz. (1 cup) softened cream cheese
1 tsp. vanilla extract
1/2 tsp. grated orange rind
3 to 4 Tbs. honey (to taste)
extra carob powder

1) Combine everything except carob powder in a small mixing bowl. Beat until fluffy and smooth.

2) Spread half the filling on one cake layer. Place the other layer on top.

3) Spread the remaining filling on top of the second layer.

4) Sift a small amount of carob powder over the top for a nicely finished surface. If the weather is hot, chill before serving.

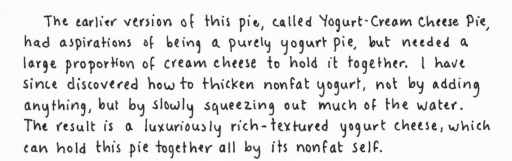

YOGURT PIE

The earlier version of this pie, called Yogurt-Cream Cheese Pie, had aspirations of being a purely yogurt pie, but needed a large proportion of cream cheese to hold it together. I have since discovered how to thicken nonfat yogurt, not by adding anything, but by slowly squeezing out much of the water. The result is a luxuriously rich-textured yogurt cheese, which can hold this pie together all by its nonfat self.

1) Place 6 layers of cheesecloth about 16 inches long in a large (12-inch diameter) colander. (If you haven't one that large, you can use 2 smaller colanders, and cut slightly shorter pieces of cheesecloth.) Place the colander(s) over a bowl or in the sink.

2) Add 2½ quarts nonfat yogurt, and wrap the cheesecloth around it tightly, securing the cloth with a clip or a bagtie.

3) Place a 3- or 4-lb. bag of beans on top, and let it sit there for 6 to 8 hours. The yogurt will solidify as its water content slowly drips out the bottom. When you unwrap it, you will find about 5 cups of thick, creamy yogurt cheese.

Preparation time:
30 minutes
plus time to chill

Yield:
5 to 6 servings

SWEET CRUMB CRUST:

2 cups crushed graham crackers or ginger snaps (easily
done in a food processor)

½ cup shredded unsweetened coconut (optional. If you prefer,
you can substitute another ½ cup crushed
graham crackers or ginger snaps.)

¼ cup finely minced pecans

6 Tbs. butter, melted

1) Preheat oven to 350°F.

2) Combine all ingredients and mix well. Press the mixture
firmly into the bottom and sides of a 9-inch pie pan, building
a handsome ½-inch ridge around the edge. You will have more

FILLING:

approximately 5 cups yogurt cheese (see p.87)
5 Tbs. sugar (or more, to taste)
1¼ tsp. vanilla extract

OPTIONAL TOPPINGS:
fresh fruit (berries, pitted cherries, sliced peaches)

1) Place the yogurt cheese in a medium-sized bowl with the sugar and vanilla, and beat lightly with a whisk until completely blended.

2) Turn into the prepared crust. Optional: top with leftover crust mixture. Cover tightly and chill. Serve plain or with a topping.

Montana's Mom's Dynamite Cheesecake

"Loved by millions from coast to coast" —Montana

Preparation time: 15 minutes

Baking time: 25 minutes, then
  a cooling period, then
  8 minutes more

Yield: enough
for 8 to 10

Basic cheesecake: unadorned and unabashed.
Make it a day ahead, so it will have plenty of time to set.
NOTE: Use a food processor or blender to make
the graham cracker crumbs.

CRUST:

2 cups graham cracker crumbs

½ stick butter or margarine, melted

~Combine, and press firmly into the bottom of a 10-inch
springform pan.

FILLING:

16 oz. (2 packages) cream cheese, softened
1/3 cup sugar
4 eggs
1 1/2 tsp. vanilla extract
3 Tbs. lemon juice
1/2 tsp. lemon rind

1) Preheat oven to 375°F.
2) Beat all filling ingredients together until smooth.
3) Pour onto crust and bake for 25 minutes, or until set.
Remove from oven and cool to room temperature. You will need
the oven again, so you can either leave it on, or reheat it.

TOPPING:

1 1/2 cups sour cream
3 Tbs. sugar
1/2 tsp. vanilla extract

1) Reheat oven to 375°F.
2) Blend topping ingredients well, and pour on top of cooled cake.
3) Bake for 8 minutes. Remove from oven and cool to room
temperature, then cover tightly (still in the pan) and chill at
least 12 hours.

Ginger·Brandy Cheesecake

Preparation time: 20 minutes
Baking time: 40 minutes

Yield: 8 to 10
servings

I. CRUST: 2 cups ginger snap crumbs (make them in a food
processor or a blender. Or the old-fashioned way,
with a rolling pin)
5 Tbs. melted butter

Mix together well. Press firmly into the bottom of a 10-inch
springform pan.

II. FILLING: 12 oz. (1½ packages) cream cheese, softened
(lowfat OK)
1½ cups sour cream or yogurt (or a combination)
4 eggs (some or all yolks can be omitted)
¼ cup honey or sugar (or, to taste)
¼ cup brandy
2 Tbs. finely grated fresh ginger
a dash of salt

1) Preheat oven to 350°F.

2) whip everything together until very smooth. Taste to adjust sweetening.

3) Pour onto the crust in the springform pan. Bake for 40 minutes, or until the center is firm to the touch and the edges are slightly brown. Cool completely before removing the rim of the pan and glazing.

III. GLAZE: 2 Tbs. cornstarch   ½ tsp. orange rind
              ¾ cup orange juice   optional: candied ginger,
              2 Tbs. honey or sugar   cut into thin strips
              1 Tbs. brandy

1) Place cornstarch in a small saucepan. Whisk in the orange juice.

2) Cook over medium heat, whisking constantly, until smooth and glossy (about 5 minutes).

3) Remove from heat, and whisk in the remaining ingredients, except the candied ginger. Pour the hot glaze onto the cooled cheesecake, spreading it evenly. If desired, decorate in an expansive pattern with strips of candied ginger. Chill thoroughly before serving.

Amaretto Cheesecake
Chocolate Cookie Crust

20 minutes to prepare
1½ hours to bake
(Plus at least 4 hours
  to cool and chill)

Yield:
8 to 10
servings

Make this a day ahead; cover tightly and chill overnight.
The amaretto flavor will ripen to perfection.

NOTE: Use a food processor with the steel blade attachment to crush
the cookies and grind the almonds for the crust.

CRUST:
1½ cups crushed chocolate wafer cookies
⅓ cup ground almonds
¼ cup Amaretto liqueur (plus more in filling)
2 Tbs. melted butter

FILLING:
- 1 lb. (2 cups) ricotta cheese (skim or part-skim OK)
- 8 oz. (1 cup) softened cream cheese (lowfat OK)
- 4 eggs (OK to delete yolks)
- 1/3 cup Amaretto liqueur
- 2/3 cup sugar or honey
- 1/4 tsp. salt
- 1/2 tsp. grated orange rind

1) Preheat oven to 325°F.

2) Combine the crust ingredients in a medium-sized bowl, and mix until well blended. Transfer to a 9- or 10-inch springform pan; press the mixture firmly into the floor of the pan.

3) Combine all the filling ingredients in a large mixing bowl. Beat for at least 3 minutes with an electric mixer at high speed. Scrape the bottom and sides of the bowl often.

4) Pour the batter into the crust-lined pan. Bake in the center of the oven for 1 hour. Turn off the oven and leave the cake in there for another 30 minutes.

5) Remove the cake from the oven and let it cool to room temperature. Cover the pan tightly with plastic wrap, and chill for at least 4 hours before serving.

✶ ✶ ✶ ✶ ✶ ✶ CHEESECAKE SOUFFLÉ ✶ ✶ ✶ ✶ ✶
w/ Strawberry~Marmalade Sauce 🍓🍓

✶ ✶

15 minutes to assemble
1 hour to bake

Yield:
about 6 servings

   Like other soufflés, this is at its best fresh from the oven. All the ingredients can be prepared ahead; make the sauce while it bakes.

NOTES: ✓ Separate the eggs ahead of time- the whites should be at room temperature.
       ✓ It's ok to use frozen unsweetened berries. (Defrost them first.)

a little butter or oil for the pan

6 egg whites, at room temperature

1 1/2 lbs. (3 cups) ricotta (skim or part-skim ok)

5 Tbs. unbleached white flour

a scant 1/2 tsp. salt

2/3 cup sifted confectioners' sugar

1 tsp. vanilla extract

1/2 tsp. grated lemon rind

1 tsp. grated orange rind

1) Preheat oven to 375°F. Lightly grease a 9- or 10-inch soufflé dish.

2) Place the egg whites in a large mixing bowl. Beat until they form stiff peaks. Don't bother cleaning the beaters.

3) Place the ricotta in another large bowl, and use the same beaters to whip it for about 5 minutes at high speed, gradually adding the flour, salt, sugar, and vanilla. Stir in the citrus rinds.

4) Gently fold the beaten egg whites into the ricotta mixture. Don't worry if the results are not perfectly uniform.

5) Turn into the prepared pan, and bake undisturbed for 1 hour. Serve hot, while it is still puffy, with the following sauce.

STRAWBERRY·MARMALADE SAUCE:

    2 1/2 cups strawberries
    1 cup orange or lemon marmalade
    optional: a few tablespoons of orange-flavored liqueur

1) Combine strawberries, marmalade, and optional liqueur in a medium-sized saucepan. Bring to a boil, then lower heat and simmer uncovered for about 10 minutes.

2) Ladle a little pool of hot or warm sauce onto each serving plate, then mound a portion of soufflé in the center. Drizzle a little extra sauce over the top. Divine!

Mandelbrot

Preparation time:
1¼ hours, total

Yield:
3½ dozen

a little butter or oil for the pan

3 eggs

½ cup light-colored honey

½ cup melted butter or canola oil

1 tsp. grated orange rind

1 tsp. vanilla extract

2¾ cups unbleached white flour

2 tsp. baking powder

½ tsp. salt

1 cup finely minced almonds

½ cup raisins or currants

½ cup minced dates (optional)

1) Preheat oven to 315°F. Lightly grease a cookie sheet.

2) In a large mixing bowl, beat together eggs, honey, and butter or oil until light and fluffy. Stir in orange rind and vanilla extract.

3) Sift the flour, baking powder, and salt into the egg mixture. Add nuts and dried fruit, and stir until well combined.

4) Divide the batter in half. Shape 2 parallel logs, each about 2 inches wide, on the cookie sheet.

5) Bake for 30 minutes. Let cool for about 15 minutes.

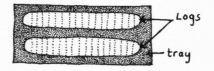

Logs

tray

6) Slice the baked logs into ½-inch pieces. Return these to the cookie sheet and bake for 15 minutes longer. Cool completely before eating.

Whole Wheat Poppy Seed Cookies

Preparation time:
45 minutes, total

NOTE: You might need
to add dough-chilling
time, if your kitchen is hot.

Yield:
4½ dozen

a little butter or oil for the pan(s)
½ cup (1 stick) butter, softened
¾ cup (packed) light brown sugar
2 eggs
½ tsp. vanilla extract
½ tsp. grated lemon rind
⅓ cup poppy seeds
1 cup unbleached white flour
1 cup whole wheat pastry flour
2 tsp. baking powder
½ tsp. salt
extra flour for rolling the dough

1) Preheat oven to 375°F. Lightly grease one or two cookie sheets.

2) Place butter and sugar in a large mixing bowl. Beat at high speed for about 3 minutes. Add eggs one at a time, beating well after each. Stir in vanilla, lemon rind, and poppy seeds.

3) Sift the flours, baking powder, and salt directly into the butter mixture. Mix by hand until completely blended. If it is hot or humid in your kitchen, wrap and refrigerate the dough for at least an hour before proceeding.

4) Flour a clean, dry surface, and roll the dough to 1/4-inch thickness. Cut into shapes, and bake for 10 to 12 minutes, or until lightly browned on the bottom. Cool for at least 10 minutes before eating.

Cashew Shortbread

Preparation time:
35 to 40 minutes, total

Yield: 4 dozen

1 cup (2 sticks) butter, softened
1/2 cup (packed) light brown sugar
3 Tbs. granulated sugar
1 cup finely minced cashews
2 cups unbleached white flour
1/2 tsp. salt
1/2 tsp. baking powder
extra flour for rolling the dough

1) Preheat oven to 375°F.

2) Place the butter and sugars in a large mixing bowl. Beat at high speed with an electric mixer for about 3 minutes. Stir in the cashews.

3) Sift the flour, salt and baking powder directly into the bowl. Use your hands to mix the dough as quickly and efficiently as possible, until it holds together.

4) Flour a clean, dry surface, and roll the dough until it is somewhere between ¼ and ½ inch thick. Cut into simple shapes and place on an ungreased cookie sheet.

5) Bake for 10 to 12 minutes, or until lightly browned on the bottom. Cool for at least 10 minutes before eating.

Rugelach

Preparation time:
1 hour, total

NOTE: You might need to add dough-chilling time, if your kitchen is hot.

Yield: 4 dozen

1 cup (2 sticks) butter, softened
1 cup cottage cheese
2 cups unbleached white flour
½ tsp. salt
extra flour for rolling the dough

FILLING:
½ cup sugar
2 tsp. cinnamon
½ cup finely minced nuts
OPTIONAL: ½ cup semisweet
   chocolate chips, ground to
   a coarse meal in a blender

COMBINE

1) Use an electric mixer or a food processor (a few short bursts with the steel blade attachment) to mix the butter, cottage cheese, flour, and salt into a uniform dough. Divide the dough into 4 equal parts, and make each one into a ball. If your kitchen is hot or humid, wrap and refrigerate each ball of dough for at least an hour before proceeding.

2) Preheat oven to 375°F.

3) Flour a clean, dry surface. Roll each ball of dough into as perfect a circle as possible, about 1/4 inch thick.

4) Sprinkle each circle with a quarter of the filling, distributing it as evenly as you can up to 1/2 inch of the rim.

5) Cut like so: (like a pizza), and roll each wedge from the outside edge of the circle toward the center.

6) Place the filled pastries on an ungreased cookie sheet. Bake for 20 to 25 minutes, or until nicely browned. Cool 10 minutes before eating.

CHOCOLATE CHIP - MINT
△ COOKIES △

The world's best holiday cookie!

• These freeze beautifully in a tightly lidded
container or a heavy zip-style plastic bag.

• Let the butter soften, unwrapped, directly in the bowl.

Preparation time:
20 minutes to assemble
12 to 15 minutes to bake

Yield:
About 4 dozen cookies

Nonstick spray for the baking tray
1½ cups (3 sticks) butter, softened in a large bowl
1 cup (packed) light brown sugar
1 cup granulated sugar
2 large eggs
2 tsp. pure vanilla extract
2 tsp. peppermint extract
3 cups unbleached all-purpose flour
½ cup unsweetened cocoa
2 tsp. baking powder
½ tsp. salt (scant measure)
One 12-oz. package semisweet chocolate chips

1) Preheat the oven to 350°F. Line two baking trays with foil or parchment, and spray with nonstick spray.

2) Add the sugars to the softened butter in the large bowl, and beat with an electric mixer at high speed until fluffy (about 3 to 5 minutes).

3) Beat in the eggs one at a time, continuing to beat until each is incorporated. Beat in the extracts with the second egg.

4) In a separate bowl, sift together the flour, cocoa, baking powder, and salt. Add this to the butter mixture, along with the chocolate chips. Stir until combined.

5) Drop the batter by rounded teaspoons onto the prepared trays, flattening each mound slightly with the back of a spoon.

6) Bake in the center of the preheated oven for 12 to 15 minutes, or until dry on the tops and slightly darkened on the bottoms. Remove from the oven, and let the cookies sit on the trays for about 5 minutes before gently transferring them to a rack to crispen. Repeat with the rest of the batter — you'll need to bake these in shifts.

Stone fruit Clafoutis

Preparation time: 15 minutes, plus 30 to 35 minutes to bake

Yield: 4 or 5 servings

A traditional dessert from the farm culture of southern France, a clafoutis ("cla-FOO-tee") is a fluffy popover-like cake, made from a thick, eggy batter studded with fruit. It's fun to bring the pan straight from the oven to the table, so everyone can admire this beautiful, dramatic-looking dish.

• In the off-season, you can use frozen unsweetened fruit, adding it to the batter without defrosting it first. You can also use canned fruit (packed in water or juice) if you drain it very well first.

• One more option: This can also be made with dried fruit that has been soaked for an hour or so in fruit juice or a fruity liqueur. If using larger pieces of fruit, slice them first.

Nonstick spray for the pan
2 to 3 Tbs. butter
1 ½ cups pitted, sliced cherries, plums, peaches and/or apricots
1 Tbs. plus 1 ⅓ cups unbleached all-purpose flour
1 ½ cups milk

2 Tbs. granulated sugar
4 large eggs
1 tsp. pure vanilla extract
1/4 tsp. salt
Powdered sugar for the top

1) Preheat the oven to 375°F. Lightly spray a 9 x 13-inch baking pan with nonstick spray, then add a small chunk (2-3 Tbs.) of butter. Place the pan in the preheating oven for a minute or so to melt the butter, then take it out and carefully tilt the pan in all directions to distribute the melted butter. Set aside.

2) In a small bowl, toss together the fruit and 1 Tbs. of the flour, and let it stand for a few minutes.

3) Pour the milk into a blender or a food processor fitted with the steel blade. Add the sugar, eggs, vanilla, and salt, and process for a few seconds. Add 1 1/3 cups flour and process until the mixture is uniformly blended. (You may need to stop and scrape the sides with a rubber spatula to get all the flour mixed in.)

4) Pour the batter into the prepared pan, spoon in the coated fruit, and bake in the center of the oven for 30 to 35 minutes, or until puffed and lightly browned.

5) Serve hot or warm, cut into large squares, and topped with powdered sugar.

GREEK-STYLE RICE PUDDING

Preparation time: 30 minutes, plus time to cool and chill
Yield: 3 to 4 servings

This is akin to a lemon custard with rice. You'll be impressed by its creaminess, especially considering that it has no milk in it.

NOTE: Juice the lemon before grating its zest. You might need 2 lemons to get enough zest, but you'll probably only need the juice from one of them.

1 2/3 cups water
1 cup uncooked white rice
1 Tbs. butter (optional)
1/4 tsp. salt (rounded measure)
2 large eggs, beaten
1/3 cup (packed) light brown sugar
1 tsp. grated lemon zest
2 Tbs. fresh lemon juice
1/2 tsp. pure vanilla extract
Cinnamon

1) Combine the water, rice, optional butter, and salt in a medium-sized saucepan. Bring to a boil, then lower the heat to the slowest possible simmer. Cover, and let it cook undisturbed for 20 minutes. At this time, test for tenderness, and cook a little longer (possibly with an additional splash of water) as necessary.

2) When the rice is tender, remove the pan from the stove, and use a fork to beat in the pre-beaten eggs. Continue beating for about a minute after the eggs are incorporated.

3) Stir in the sugar, lemon zest, lemon juice, and vanilla. Transfer to a bowl.

4) Sprinkle the top generously with cinnamon, then cool to room temperature. Cover tightly and refrigerate until cold.

APPLESAUCE ~ COCOA SPICE CAKE

Preparation time: 25 to 30 minutes to assemble
45 to 55 minutes to bake

Yield: 1 large cake (12 or more servings)

NOTES:
- If you prefer this sweeter, increase the sugar to 2 cups.
- Let the butter soften, unwrapped, directly in the bowl.
- Use a food processor fitted with the steel blade to grind the walnuts into a coarse powder. It will only take a few brief spurts.

Nonstick spray for the pan
3/4 cup (1 1/2 sticks) butter, softened in a large bowl
1 1/2 cups (packed) dark brown sugar
2 large eggs
1 Tbs. pure vanilla extract
1 tsp. grated orange zest
3 cups unbleached all-purpose flour
1/2 cup unsweetened cocoa
1/2 tsp salt
2 tsp. baking powder
1 tsp. baking soda
1 1/2 tsp. cinnamon
1/2 tsp. allspice or ground cloves

½ tsp. nutmeg
1 cup finely ground walnuts
1½ cups unsweetened applesauce
½ cup buttermilk or plain yogurt

1) Preheat the oven to 350°F. Spray the interior and tube of a standard-size tube pan with nonstick spray.

2) Add the sugar to the softened butter in the large bowl, and beat until fluffy with an electric mixer (or wildly by hand). Add the eggs one at a time, beating well after each.

3) Stir in the vanilla and orange zest. Set aside.

4) In a second large bowl, sift together the dry ingredients, then stir in the ground walnuts.

5) In a third, smaller bowl, whisk together the applesauce and buttermilk or yogurt until well blended.

6) Add the dry ingredients and the applesauce mixture alternately to the butter mixture (dry-wet–dry-wet-dry). Stir just enough to blend after each addition.

7) Transfer the batter to the prepared pan, spreading it evenly into place. Bake in the center of the preheated oven for 45 to 55 minutes, or until a sharp knife inserted all the way into the center comes out clean. Cool for at least 30 minutes before removing from the pan and serving.

Hazelnut Torte _with_ Raspberry-Studded Orange Glaze

Preparation time: 1 hour and
20 minutes, including
baking and glazing

Yield:
6 to 8 servings

· Separate the eggs a few hours ahead of time, so
  they can come to room temperature.

6 large eggs
Nonstick spray for the pan
1 cup powdered sugar (sifted into the measuring cup)
3 Tbs. fresh lemon juice
¼ tsp. salt
1 Tbs. grated orange zest
¼ cup unbleached all-purpose flour
1 cup finely ground hazelnuts

GLAZE:
1 Tbs. cornstarch
2 Tbs. granulated sugar
¼ cup orange juice
1 Tbs. fruity liqueur (optional)
A handful or two beautiful fresh raspberries

1) (Do this ahead): Separate the eggs, placing the yolks and whites in two large bowls. Cover each bowl tightly with plastic wrap and allow to come to room temperature.

2) Preheat the oven to 350°F. Generously spray the inside bottom of a 9-inch springform pan with nonstick spray.

3) Beat the egg whites at high speed with an electric mixer until they form stiff peaks. Set aside.

4) Without cleaning the beaters, begin beating the yolks at medium speed. Gradually add the powdered sugar, lemon juice, and salt. Continue beating for another 3 to 5 minutes, or until lemony in color.

5) Use a rubber spatula and a gentle, turning motion to fold the orange zest, flour, and ground nuts into the yolk mixture.

6) Add the beaten egg whites, using the same rubber spatula and turning action—and scraping from the bottom of the bowl—to fold the whites into the thicker mixture. Try to blend everything as uniformly as possible without deflating the egg whites. It will be imperfect. (Better to undermix than to overdo it.)

7) Turn the batter into the prepared pan. Bake for 35 minutes in the center of the oven, then transfer the pan to a rack, and allow the torte to cool to room temperature before removing the rim of the pan.

8) Meanwhile, combine the cornstarch and granulated sugar in a small saucepan. Drizzle in the orange juice and optional liqueur, whisking constantly until the cornstarch dissolves.

9) Continue to whisk as you cook the mixture over medium-low heat until thick and glossy. This should take 3 to 5 minutes.

10) Spread the hot glaze over the top of the cooled torte. Decorate with the raspberries, and serve.

INDEX

Ten Speed Press
PO Box 7123
Berkeley, California 94707
www.tenspeed.com

Distributed in Australia by Simon and Schuster Australia, in Canada by Ten Speed Press Canada, in New Zealand by Southern Publishers Group, in South Africa by Real Books, and in the United Kingdom and Europe by Publishers Group UK.

Cover and text design by Nancy Austin and Colleen Cain
Handlettering, frontispiece, and illustrations by Mollie Katzen

Library of Congress Cataloging-in-Publication Data

Katzen, Mollie, 1950-
 Mollie Katzen's recipes : desserts / by Mollie Katzen.
     p. cm.
 Includes index.
 Summary: "A collection of 50 hand-lettered dessert recipes from the author of
the Moosewood Cookbook, in a compact easel format"—Provided by publisher.
 ISBN 978-1-58008-879-4
 1. Desserts. I. Title.
 TX773.K3345 2009
 641.8'6—dc22

                              2008038993

Printed in China
First printing, 2009
1 2 3 4 5 6 7 8 9 10 — 13 12 11 10 09